# SPEEDIEST!

## 19 VERY FAST ANIMALS

## STEVE JENKINS

HOUGHTON MIFFLIN HARCOURT · BOSTON · NEW YORK

# Speediest!

## Contents

## Move!

Predators are animals that eat other animals. Some of these hunters are sneaky. They wait for prey to come close, and then they pounce. Others make traps or use deadly venom. But many predators rely on speed to get a meal. They are faster than their prey.

Animals that can be food for another creature have their own ways of staying safe. Some are good at hiding. Others are poisonous or protected by armor or spines. But many escape danger by being quick.

This book is about these fast animals—some of the speediest on earth.

*Words in blue can be found in the glossary on page 38.*

Some animals use
their speed to catch
and eat other animals.

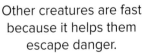

Other creatures are fast
because it helps them
escape danger.

# Fastest runner

Many of the grazing animals that live on the plains of Africa are fast. But the **cheetah** is speedier. It can run faster than any other animal. It hunts gazelles and other antelopes, and uses its speed to chase them down.

**Where it lives**
Central and southern Africa

**What it eats**
Antelopes, small animals

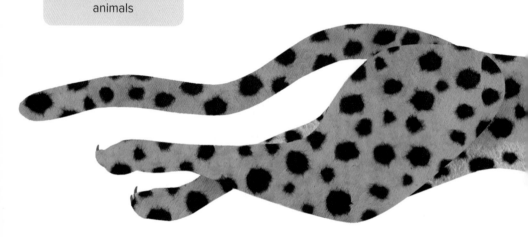

The cheetah must change direction quickly as it chases its prey. This cat's heavy tail helps it keep its balance.

TOP SPEED
70 mph*
113 kph*

*mph = miles per hour
*kph = kilometers per hour

It takes a lot of energy to run fast, and the cheetah can only keep up its top speed for a minute or so.

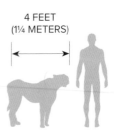

4 FEET
(1¼ METERS)

At top speed, the cheetah covers 23 feet (7 meters) with every stride.

30 feet (9 meters)

Distance covered in one second by a fast human runner

100 feet (30 meters)

Distance covered in one second by a cheetah

# Who needs to fly?

The **ostrich** is the largest bird in the world. It can't fly, but it can run as fast as a racehorse. The ostrich will try to escape danger by running away. If it can't escape, it defends itself with a kick that is strong enough to kill a lion.

**Where it lives**
Central and southern Africa

**What it eats**
Fruit, seeds, leaves, insects, frogs, lizards, other small animals

A chicken egg and an ostrich egg. The ostrich lays the largest egg of any animal.

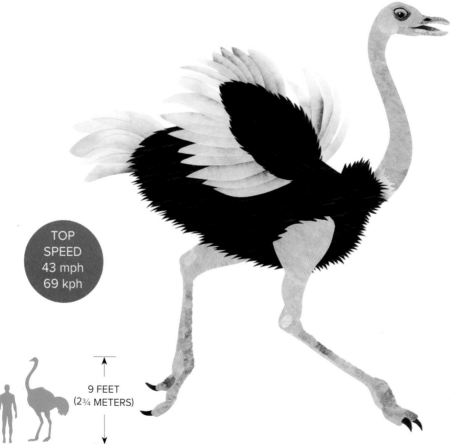

TOP SPEED
43 mph
69 kph

9 FEET
(2¾ METERS)

# Small but speedy

The **Australian tiger beetle** is one of the world's fastest animals for its size. This speedy insect is a deadly predator. It runs down its prey and tears it to pieces with its sharp jaws.

**Where it lives**
Australia

**What it eats**
Insects and spiders

This beetle can travel 170 times the length of its body in one second.

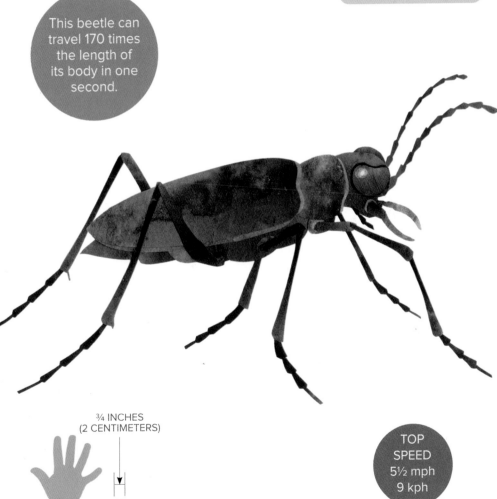

¾ INCHES
(2 CENTIMETERS)

TOP SPEED
5½ mph
9 kph

## A quick escape

The **brown hare** has long, powerful legs. It uses them to escape danger. This hare can outrun foxes and most other predators. Hares are related to rabbits, but they are larger and have longer legs.

Hares change color from brown or gray in the summer to white in the winter.

TOP SPEED
45 mph
72 kph

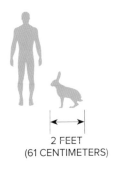

2 FEET
(61 CENTIMETERS)

**Where it lives**
Europe and western Asia

**What it eats**
Grass, grain, seeds, twigs, bark

# Fleet feet

The **greater roadrunner** can fly, but it would rather run. It can run faster than any other flying bird. Its speed helps it escape danger and chase down its prey.

Only a few flightless birds, such as the ostrich, can run faster than the roadrunner.

TOP
SPEED
20 mph
32 kph

22 INCHES
(56 CENTIMETERS)

The greater roadrunner can fly for only a short distance.

**Where it lives**
Southwest United States, northern Mexico

**What it eats**
Lizards, snakes, scorpions, rodents, insects

# Running on water

The **green basilisk lizard** is found in the trees of the rainforest. It stays close to streams or ponds. If there is danger, this lizard can drop from a branch and run across the surface of the water. It can travel about 15 feet (4½ meters) before it begins to sink. But it is a good swimmer and can often paddle to safety.

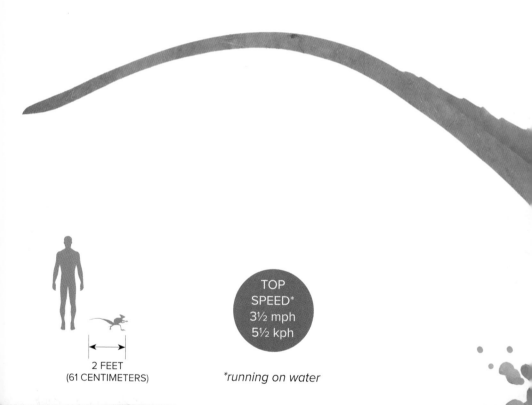

2 FEET
(61 CENTIMETERS)

TOP
SPEED*
3½ mph
5½ kph

*running on water

The green basilisk's long toes and quick legs help it stay on top of the water.

**Where it lives**
Central and South America

**What it eats**
Plants, insects, small animals

The basilisk lizard is nicknamed the "Jesus Christ lizard."

## Fast fish

The **sailfish** swims faster than any creature in the sea. It charges into a school of smaller fish and stabs or stuns them with its long bill. Sometimes sailfish work together. They herd the fish into a ball, then attack them.

TOP
SPEED
68 mph
109 kph

**Where it lives**
Warm ocean waters worldwide

**What it eats**
Fish and squid

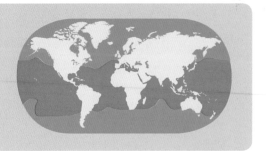

The sailfish raises the big fin on its back to make itself look larger.

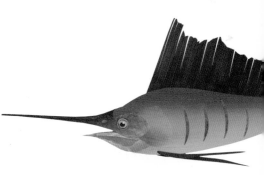

The sailfish confuses its prey or signals other sailfish by changing its color.

11 FEET
(3½ METERS)

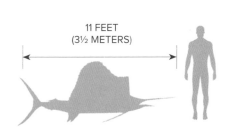

## Ten-armed devil

The **Humboldt squid** is one of the top predators in its habitat. It is fast, and has good eyesight and strong tentacles. The Humboldt squid is a flying squid. It can jet out of the water and sail through the air. It is one of the smartest and fastest invertebrates in the world.

TOP
SPEED
15 mph
24 kph

7 FEET
(213 CENTIMETERS)

Humboldt squid travel in shoals, or groups, of more than 1,000 animals.

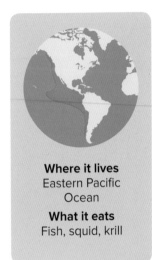

**Where it lives**
Eastern Pacific Ocean

**What it eats**
Fish, squid, krill

Mexican fishermen have nicknamed this squid "red devil."

The Humboldt squid is bioluminescent—it can produce its own light. It changes color to communicate with other squid.

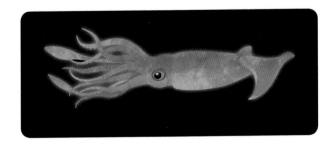

This swift spends most of its life in the air. It even eats, drinks, and sleeps in flight.

## Life in the sky

The **spine-tailed swift** is a fast and graceful flier. In a dive, it is one of the speediest animals on earth. It is also one of the fastest birds in level flight.

TOP SPEED*
69 mph
111 kph

*\* in level flight*

8 INCHES
(20 CENTIMETERS)

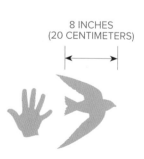

**Where it lives**
China, Japan, eastern Australia

**What it eats**
Flying insects

# Airborne!

Many fish try to escape danger by swimming fast. The **flying fish** can also swim fast, but it has a better trick. It swims at top speed and bursts from the surface. In the air, it spreads its winglike fins and glides, leaving most predators behind.

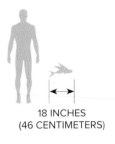

18 INCHES
(46 CENTIMETERS)

TOP
SPEED
43 mph
69 kph

Flying fish can glide above the surface for more than 650 feet (198 meters).

**Where it lives**
Tropical and semi-tropical oceans worldwide

**What it eats**
Plankton, small marine animals

## Fastest of all

The **peregrine falcon** is the fastest animal on earth. It hunts by diving at high speed and striking a bird or bat in midair. Its victim is stunned or killed. The peregrine falcon snatches its prey as it falls and carries it to its nest.

TOP SPEED
200 mph
322 kph

The dive of the peregrine falcon is called a "stoop."

18 INCHES
(46 CENTIMETERS)

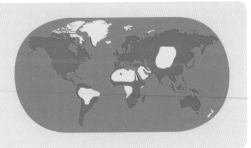

**Where it lives**
Every continent
except Antarctica
**What it eats**
Other birds, bats

Young peregrine falcons practice hunting. One bird pretends to be the prey while the other bird attacks. They are careful to not hurt each other.

## Flying dragon

The **common green darner dragonfly** is one of the world's fastest insects. It is also a fierce hunter. It captures butterflies, moths, and other dragonflies and eats them in midair.

Dragonflies can hover and fly backwards as well as forward.

TOP SPEED
35 mph
56 kph

3 INCHES
(7½ CENTIMETERS)

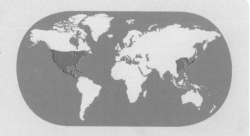

**Where it lives**
United States, Southern Canada, Central America, Japan, and China

**What it eats**
Flying insects

24

# The fastest flier

Bats are swift and agile fliers. The fastest of these airborne mammals is the **Mexican free-tailed bat**. The peregrine falcon is faster in a dive, but this little bat is speedier than any bird in level flight.

**Where it lives**
North and South America

**What it eats**
Moths and other flying insects

This bat can consume its body weight in insects every night.

TOP SPEED
100 mph
161 kph

One Mexican free-tailed bat colony in Texas contains more than 20 million bats. The bats leave their cave in the evening to hunt for insects.

11 INCHES
(28 CENTIMETERS)

# Deadly slither

The **black mamba** is the longest venomous snake in Africa. It's also the fastest snake in the world. It can crawl as fast as most people can run—a scary thought. These snakes usually avoid humans, but they are dangerous if they feel threatened.

The bite of a black mamba can kill a person in less than 30 minutes.

TOP SPEED 12 mph 19 kph

The skin of the black mamba is actually brown. This snake gets its name from the black color of its mouth, which it opens when it senses danger.

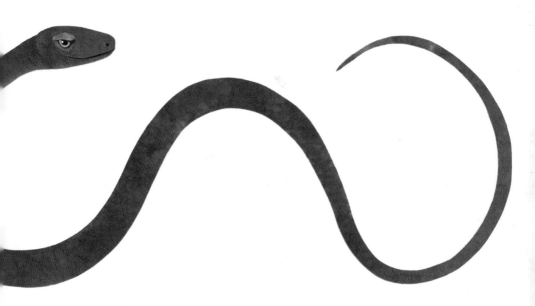

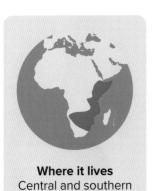

**Where it lives**
Central and southern Africa

**What it eats**
Birds, bats, other small mammals

14 FEET
(4¼ METERS)

# Leaps and bounds

The **red kangaroo** is the largest kangaroo. It is also the world's biggest marsupial. Kangaroos have an unusual walk. They balance on their front legs and tail, then bring their back legs forward. Kangaroos move quickly by taking big hops with their powerful back legs.

A red kangaroo can leap 30 feet (9 meters) in a single bound).

**Where it lives**
Australia
**What it eats**
Grasses and shrubs

6 FEET
(183 CENTIMETERS)

TOP
SPEED
40 mph
64 kph

The kangaroo
is the only large
animal that moves
by hopping.

30 feet (9 meters)

The kangaroo's leap compared to a human

# Burrowing beast

The name **aardvark** means "earth pig."
The aardvark's powerful legs and sharp
claws make it one of the world's fastest
diggers. It also uses its claws to tear
open ant and termite nests. It slurps up
the insects with a long, sticky tongue.

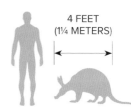

4 FEET
(1¼ METERS)

An aardvark
can eat as many
as 50,000 ants
or termites in one
night.

TOP
SPEED
8 fpm*
2½ mpm*

burrowing speed:
*fpm = feet per minute
*mpm= meters per minute

**Where it lives**
Central and southern
Africa

**What it eats**
Ants, termites, plant
roots

# Swinger

The **gibbon** travels through the forest by swinging from branch to branch. It can move through the treetops at an amazing speed. Like all apes, the gibbon has long arms and no tail. It also has a special wrist joint that helps it grasp tree branches.

**Where it lives**
Southeast Asia

**What it eats**
Leaves, seeds, flowers, insects, bird eggs, small birds

A gibbon can leap 50 feet (15 meters) from branch to branch.

3 FEET
(91 CENTIMETERS)

TOP SPEED*
35 mph
56 kph

*swinging through
the trees

Gibbons often walk on two feet when they are on the ground.

# Knockout punch

The **mantis shrimp** stuns or kills its prey with a blow from its clublike claw. Its strike is one of the fastest movements in the animal world. A blow from this shrimp's claw can shatter a clam shell—or the glass of an aquarium.

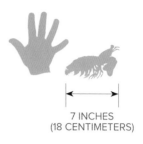

7 INCHES
(18 CENTIMETERS)

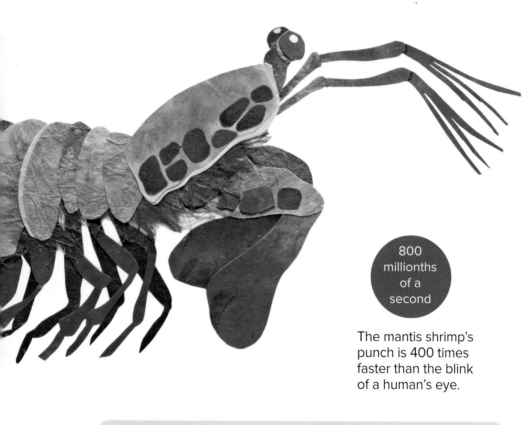

**800 millionths of a second**

The mantis shrimp's punch is 400 times faster than the blink of a human's eye.

**Where it lives**
Coastal waters of eastern Africa, Southeast Asia, and Australia

**What it eats**
Clams, shrimp, fish, worms

# Snap!

The animal world record for speed belongs to the **Panamanian termite**. It holds its jaws pressed tightly together. If it is in danger, it snaps them closed. This motion is extremely fast. It creates a shock wave that can stun or kill an attacker.

25 millionths of a second

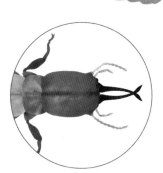

The ready position (above) and after a jaw snap (left). This termite's jaw snap is thousands of times faster than a human eye blink.

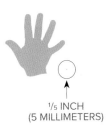

¹/₅ INCH
(5 MILLIMETERS)

**Where it lives**
Central America, northern South America
**What it eats**
Wood and dead plant material

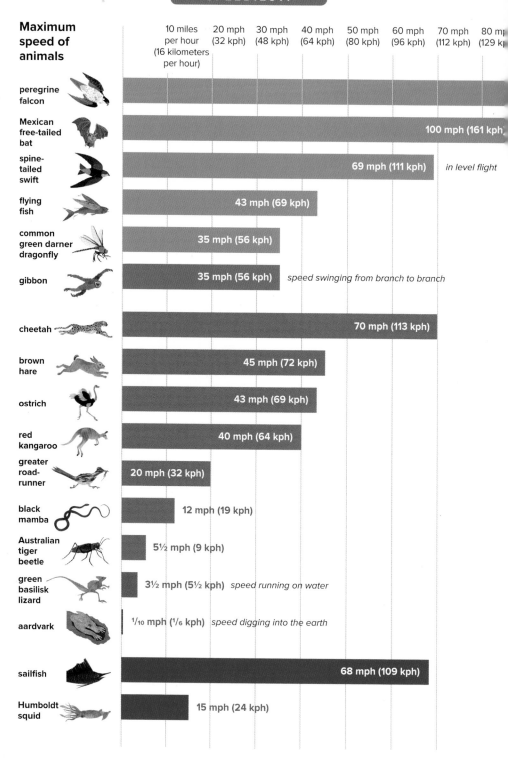

# Maximum speed of animals

| | 10 miles per hour (16 kilometers per hour) | 20 mph (32 kph) | 30 mph (48 kph) | 40 mph (64 kph) | 50 mph (80 kph) | 60 mph (96 kph) | 70 mph (112 kph) | 80 mph (129 kph) |
|---|---|---|---|---|---|---|---|---|

**peregrine falcon**

**Mexican free-tailed bat** — 100 mph (161 kph)

**spine-tailed swift** — 69 mph (111 kph) *in level flight*

**flying fish** — 43 mph (69 kph)

**common green darner dragonfly** — 35 mph (56 kph)

**gibbon** — 35 mph (56 kph) *speed swinging from branch to branch*

**cheetah** — 70 mph (113 kph)

**brown hare** — 45 mph (72 kph)

**ostrich** — 43 mph (69 kph)

**red kangaroo** — 40 mph (64 kph)

**greater road-runner** — 20 mph (32 kph)

**black mamba** — 12 mph (19 kph)

**Australian tiger beetle** — 5½ mph (9 kph)

**green basilisk lizard** — 3½ mph (5½ kph) *speed running on water*

**aardvark** — ¹/₁₀ mph (¹/₆ kph) *speed digging into the earth*

**sailfish** — 68 mph (109 kph)

**Humboldt squid** — 15 mph (24 kph)

| 100 mph (161 kph) | 110 mph (177 kph) | 120 mph (193 kph) | 130 mph (209 kph) | 140 mph (225 kph) | 150 mph (241 kph) | 160 mph (257 kph) | 170 mph (274 kph) | 180 mph (290 kph) | 190 mph (306 kph) | 200 mph (322 kph) |
|---|---|---|---|---|---|---|---|---|---|---|

**200 mph (322 kph)**

The **Australian tiger beetle** is one of the fastest animals in the world for its size. If a human could run as fast as this beetle relative to her size, she'd be moving at more than 600 miles per hour (966 kilometers per hour).

---

### Fast movements in the animal world

**mantis shrimp**
The mantis shrimp's claw strike is almost 400 times faster than a human eye blink.

**Panamanian termite**
This termite's jaw snap, which the termite uses to defend its nest, is 12,000 times faster than an eye blink.

A human eye blink lasts about 3/10 of a second.

## Glossary

**agile**
Quick and graceful.

**airborne**
Moving through the air.

**bill**
In the sailfish, a long, bony extension of the upper jaw.

**bioluminescent**
Light produced by a living organism. Also called "cold light."

**consume**
To eat.

**flightless**
Unable to fly. Usually refers to birds or insects.

**gazelle**
A small, graceful antelope.

**grazing**
Feeding on grass or leaves.

**habitat**
The area where an animal is naturally found. For example: grasslands, rainforests, marshes, or deserts.

**invertebrates**
Animals without a backbone.

**marsupial**
Mammals that raise their babies in a pouch.

**poisonous**
In the animal world, a creature with poison in its skin or flesh. It must be handled or eaten to cause harm.

**predator**
An animal that kills and eats other animals.

**prey**
An animal hunted and eaten by a predator.

**racehorse**
A horse especially bred to race. The fastest racehorses average more than 43 miles per hour (69 kilometers per hour) over a 440-yard (402-meter) race course.

**rainforest**
Dense forests that average more than 80 inches (2 meters) of rainfall each year.

**shoal**
A group, or school, of fish or squid.

**shock wave**
A sudden change in pressure that moves through air or water. Shock waves can be caused by an impact or explosion.

**tentacle**
A long, thin, flexible part of an animal's body. It may be used for moving, grasping something, or delivering a venomous sting.

**venom**
A poisonous fluid produced by animals as a predatory or defensive weapon.

**venomous**
In animals, a creature that injects venom with teeth, fangs, spines, or stingers.

## Bibliography

*Animal.* Edited by David Burnie & Don E. Wilson. Dorling Kindersley, 2001.

*Animal Records.* By Mark Carwardine. Sterling, 2008.

*The Book of Comparisons.* By The Diagram Group. Sidgwick & Jackson, 1980.

*The Encyclopedia of Animals.* Edited by Dr. Per Christiansen. Amber Books, 2006.

*Runners, Sliders, Bouncers, Climbers.* By Nick Bantock and Stacie Strong. Intervisual Books, 1992.

*Super Nature Encyclopedia.* By Derek Harvey. Dorling Kindersley, 2012.

*Unusual Creatures.* By Michael Hearst. Chronicle Books, 2012.

*The Usborne World of Animals.* By Susanna Davidson and Mike Unwin. Usborne Publishing, 2005.

*The Way Nature Works.* Edited by Jill Bailey. Macmillan Publishing Company, 1997.

*Wildlife of the World.* By DK Publishing. Dorling Kindersley, 2015.

## For Robin

The illustrations in this book were created as torn- and cut-paper collage.
The text type is set in Proxima Nova and New Century Schoolbook.
The display type is set in Geometric.

ISBN: 978-0-544-93710-9 hardcover
ISBN: 978-1-328-84196-4 paperback

Manufactured in China
SCP 10 9 8 7 6 5 4 3 2 1
4500696938

LEXILE: 820
F&P: P